Original title:
Holding On

Copyright © 2024 Swan Charm
All rights reserved.

Author: Olivia Oja
ISBN HARDBACK: 978-9916-79-251-3
ISBN PAPERBACK: 978-9916-79-252-0
ISBN EBOOK: 978-9916-79-253-7

The Celestial Anchor

In shadows deep, we seek the light,
A guiding star, our souls ignite.
With faith as firm as ocean's tide,
In love's embrace, we shall abide.

Through tempests fierce, our spirits soar,
A sacred bond, forevermore.
From heights above, the angels sing,
In unity, our prayers take wing.

Illuminated by Trust

A heart laid bare, in quiet grace,
Through trials faced, we find our place.
In whispered prayers, we speak our truth,
With every step, we claim our youth.

Each moment blessed, in His embrace,
With faith as armor, we run the race.
Together bound, in sacred trust,
In love's pure light, it is a must.

Residing in the Blessed

In quiet fields where spirits roam,
We find our haven, our true home.
With every breath, a sacred sigh,
In love's embrace, we learn to fly.

The gentle breeze, a soft refrain,
Reminds us of our holy gain.
In tranquil hearts, God's whispers dwell,
Reside in peace, where all is well.

The Heart's Refuge

When storms of doubt begin to rise,
We seek the warmth of tender ties.
In faith's cocoon, our hearts find peace,
As love sustains, our fears release.

A beacon bright in darkest night,
In gentle hands, we find our light.
Through joy and pain, our spirits grow,
In this safe space, our love will flow.

The Ties That Bind the Soul

In stillness, hearts unite in prayer,
With sacred whispers filling the air.
Like tendrils of light, they intertwine,
Binding the essence, the divine design.

Through trials faced and burdens borne,
With faith intact, a spirit reborn.
In every struggle, each tear we find,
The ties that bind, forever aligned.

In fellowship's warmth, our souls take flight,
Illuminated paths in the darkest night.
Together we wander, hand in hand,
In love's embrace, united we stand.

Embracing Eternal Promises

In dawn's soft glow, His promise unfolds,
A story of love, in whispers told.
With every heartbeat, we rise anew,
Embraced by grace, in glory's hue.

Through valleys low and mountains high,
His word, our strength, our spirits fly.
The vow He made, forever true,
In sacred trust, we're born anew.

With open hearts, we seek the light,
In each moment, a chance to ignite.
For all He has promised, we hold tight,
As stars in the heavens, burn ever bright.

When Hope Clings to Shadows

In shadows deep, where silence dwells,
Hope lingers soft, like sacred bells.
When doubts arise and darkness creeps,
In whispered prayers, the spirit leaps.

A flicker of light through clouds so gray,
In heartache's grip, we yearn to stay.
Yet, in His arms, all fears take flight,
Embracing the dawn beyond the night.

Through fleeting moments, our truths align,
In every challenge, His love we find.
For when despair seeks to take a hold,
We weave our faith, a tapestry bold.

Threads of Divine Assurance

In woven threads, His love reveals,
A tapestry of hope, the heart feels.
Each strand adorned with colors bright,
A promise cherished in the divine light.

With every stitch, our stories blend,
In unity found, our spirits mend.
Through every trial, His hand does guide,
With threads of assurance, we abide.

In moments shared, His presence glows,
A quiet strength as the spirit grows.
In faith we trust, in love we sigh,
With threads of grace, we learn to fly.

Cherished Bonds of the Spirit

In the quiet whispers of the night,
Our hearts connect, pure and bright.
Bound by faith, love's embrace,
We walk together, a holy grace.

Stronger than the passing time,
These ties, a sacred rhyme.
Through trials, joys, we find our song,
In unity, we truly belong.

With every prayer, our spirits rise,
To the heavens, where peace lies.
Hand in hand, we find our way,
In cherished bonds, we shall stay.

A tapestry of grace we weave,
In the heart of those who believe.
Together in spirit, we shine and glow,
With love as the seed, our souls will grow.

So let us gather, one and all,
For in His love, we shall not fall.
Together we honor what is true,
In cherished bonds, I stand with you.

The Light That Guides Our Way

When shadows gather, we seek the light,
A guiding star, pure and bright.
Through storms and trials, we have found,
The sacred glow that wraps around.

With every step, faith leads us on,
A beacon shining at each dawn.
In moments dark, we hold it near,
The light of hope, our hearts will steer.

Wherever we wander, together we go,
Trusting the love that forever flows.
The paths may twist and lead us astray,
But in His warmth, we shall not sway.

In times of doubt, lift your gaze,
For faith ignites the brightest rays.
Across the valleys, through the fray,
The light of love will guide our way.

Together we stand, in harmony,
Embracing the light, forever free.
With every heartbeat, our spirits sing,
In the light of love, we find our wing.

Beneath the Wings of Serenity

In the stillness, peace draws near,
Beneath the wings, there's no fear.
A gentle touch from up above,
Wraps us in eternal love.

When the world is heavy, hearts may ache,
In quiet moments, let us awake.
With open arms, we feel the grace,
The sacred shelter, a warm embrace.

In nature's beauty, we find our rest,
Underneath the sky, truly blessed.
The whispers of the stars align,
In the folds of love, our spirits shine.

So let us gather, hand in hand,
In the tranquil spaces of this land.
Beneath the wings, we find our way,
In serenity's arms, let us stay.

Together we breathe, in holy trust,
With hope as our guide, in love we must.
For in this calm, we clearly see,
Beneath the wings, we are truly free.

The Sacred Clasp of Belief

In the morning light, we rise and pray,
Seeking guidance for the day.
With hearts aflame, we clasp with grace,
The sacred truth in every place.

In trials faced, and sorrows borne,
Through the darkest nights, we are reborn.
With every promise, we stand so tall,
In the clasp of faith, we'll never fall.

We journey forth, with love to share,
Embracing kindness, everywhere.
In unity, our spirits blend,
With the sacred clasp, we shall ascend.

As candles flicker, a glowing sign,
Together we walk, hand in divine.
For in each other, our hopes align,
In the clasp of belief, our souls entwine.

So let us gather, hearts aglow,
In the warmth of faith, let love flow.
Together we rise, forever strong,
In the sacred clasp, where we belong.

In the Embrace of Grace

In the stillness, whispers flow,
Grace descends, a gentle glow.
Hearts awaken, spirits rise,
Beneath the vast, eternal skies.

Faith wraps round like a warm shawl,
In the shadows, He hears our call.
Love envelops, soft and wide,
With every tear, He walks beside.

Hope ignites in darkest night,
Guiding us toward the light.
In His arms, we find our place,
Lost in the embrace of grace.

Hands together, we unite,
Voices raise in joyful plight.
With each promise, our hearts sing,
In His love, eternal spring.

Every sorrow melts away,
In His love, we find the way.
Journey onward, spirits soar,
In the embrace, forevermore.

The Anchored Heart

When storms arrive and shadows loom,
The anchored heart finds peace and bloom.
Tides may rise, the winds may blow,
But deep within, our faith will grow.

In the storm's eye, calm prevails,
Through trials faced, His love unveils.
Roots run deep, our foundation strong,
In His strength, we all belong.

Amidst the turmoil, we take pause,
Reflecting on His holy cause.
With every breath, we seek the true,
In the anchored heart, love breaks through.

Harmony weaves through every pain,
Together we'll rise, not in vain.
In unity, we lift our voice,
In the anchored heart, we rejoice.

When light breaks through and shadows fade,
In His promise, we are remade.
Forever steadfast, we shall part,
In faith and love, the anchored heart.

Touch of Celestial Love

The morning light, a sacred grace,
A touch of love we can't replace.
In gentle whispers, He imparts,
The warmth that cradles longing hearts.

Through valleys low and mountains high,
His presence shines, the sweetest sigh.
Each moment blessed, each breath a gift,
In every trial, our spirits lift.

Stars above, a guiding flame,
In celestial love, we praise His name.
With open arms, the heavens call,
To dwell in peace and never fall.

In every tear, His comfort near,
A promise made, we hold so dear.
With faith as wings, our hearts ascend,
In touch of love that knows no end.

Together we walk on paths of light,
In His embrace, we find our might.
With every heartbeat, love's refrain,
A touch of heaven, here we'll reign.

Guardian Hands of Mercy

In the quiet, mercy flows,
Guardian hands, where faith bestows.
Under shadows, grace will weave,
In His arms, we must believe.

Through every trial, His strength we crave,
The heart of love, it gently saves.
When burdens weigh, we lift our eyes,
Guardian hands, where hope resides.

Every moment, sweet and rare,
In the love that fills the air.
With tender care, He leads the way,
Guardian hands, our light of day.

In every sorrow, find your way,
Trust the hands that will not sway.
For in the dark, His mercy glows,
A beacon bright, our spirit knows.

Together strong, we walk as one,
In His mercy, battles won.
With grateful hearts, we sing in throng,
In guardian hands, we all belong.

Threads of Sanctuary

In the hush of twilight's grace,
We find solace in sacred space.
Heaven's whispers gently weave,
Threads of peace for hearts that grieve.

Bound by love, we lift our voice,
In faith, we make a holy choice.
With every prayer, we feel the light,
Guiding us through the darkest night.

Each thread a story, woven tight,
A tapestry of pure delight.
In trials faced, we stand as one,
In unity, our fears undone.

Hope's fabric stitched with care,
Together, we rise above despair.
In the warmth of each embrace,
We find our true and sacred place.

Casting shadows far away,
We surrender to the light of day.
In every heartbeat, love's refrain,
Threads of sanctuary remain.

The Strength of Belief

In valleys low, where shadows fall,
The strength of belief will call.
Anchored deep in hearts that seek,
In trials faced, we shall not weak.

Mountains rise, yet we stand tall,
With faith as our unyielding wall.
Hands intertwined, we share one plea,
In unity, we find the key.

Through storms that test our fragile soul,
Belief remains our steadfast goal.
Like rivers flowing to the sea,
Our spirits soar, forever free.

Each step we take, a path divine,
In every doubt, His love we find.
With courage borne from sacred trust,
We rise again, and rise we must.

In moments brief, we pause and pray,
The strength of belief lights our way.
Through trials faced, we'll always soar,
In faith, forever we restore.

Sacred Attachment

In the fabric of love, a bond is spun,
Two hearts entwined, forever one.
In sacred moments, we find our place,
Held in the light of divine grace.

With every laugh, with every tear,
Our hearts in rhythm, truly near.
The strength of loyalty, pure and true,
In every challenge, we'll break through.

In whispered prayers, our spirits blend,
An everlasting love, without end.
Through trials faced and fears cast away,
In sacred attachment, we find our way.

Hand in hand, we bravely tread,
With faith as our guide, no words left unsaid.
In the warmth of love's embrace,
We journey forth, a holy race.

With each sunrise, our spirits dance,
In every heartbeat, a sacred chance.
With every step, we'll always strive,
In the bond of love, we are alive.

Whispers of Eternity

In twilight's glow, the stars align,
Whispers of eternity divine.
In sacred silence, the heart can hear,
Echoes of love that draw us near.

The moonlight casts a silver glow,
Guiding our souls where spirits flow.
In the stillness, we find our peace,
As the burdens of life slowly cease.

Every heartbeat, a sacred sigh,
In breath so soft, we learn to fly.
With hope's embrace, we reach for sky,
In whispers shared, we never die.

Through timeless realms, our spirits yearn,
In love's warm light, we brightly burn.
In the tapestry of night so vast,
Whispers of eternity hold us fast.

With every prayer, our hopes ascend,
In the dance of time, we find no end.
In unity bound, forever free,
We glimpse the divine, you and me.

Chains of Sacred Remembrance

In shadows deep, we lift our voice,
Bound by love, we have no choice.
Each prayer a link, a sacred chain,
Binding hearts through joy and pain.

In whispers soft, the echoes call,
From ancient times, we stand tall.
Memories dance in the light of grace,
Each story woven, a holy space.

We gather strength from days of yore,
Each moment cherished, forever more.
Through trials faced, our spirits grow,
In unity's light, our faith will show.

With every tear, a lesson learned,
In silent nights, our hearts have burned.
We seek the path where wisdom leads,
In sacred chains, our spirit feeds.

So let us rise, hand in hand,
With gratitude for this blessed land.
The sacred ties we will defend,
In remembrance' glow, love will transcend.

The Promised Land of Compassion

In fields of grace, where mercy flows,
A promised land, where kindness grows.
With open heart, we take our stand,
Together in this sacred band.

Through trials faced, we find our peace,
In every soul, love's sweet release.
Compassion blooms in hearts so wide,
In unity, we shall abide.

With every step along this path,
We break the chains of wrath and wrath.
Hope rises like the morning sun,
In every shadow, light begun.

From every corner, let us share,
The gift of love, the weight we bear.
In whispered prayers, we make a plea,
For peace to reign, for hearts to be free.

So let us walk, side by side,
In this promised land, our hearts reside.
For compassion's bond will ever last,
As we journey forth, our spirits cast.

The Flow of Spiritual Continuity

In rivers deep, the spirit flows,
Eternal streams where wisdom grows.
With every wave, a lesson learned,
In currents strong, our souls are turned.

Through mountains high and valleys wide,
In every breath, the truth abides.
From ancient roots, our hopes extend,
In unity's spirit, we will transcend.

Like seasons change, yet ever near,
The pulse of faith, it calls us here.
Through trials faced and joys embraced,
In every heart, the light's encased.

In quiet moments, the whispers rise,
Of love divine that never dies.
Through every storm, we stand as one,
In flow of grace, our journey's begun.

So let us strive to understand,
In spiritual ties, together we stand.
For in this flow, we find our way,
As light descends, we'll never sway.

Surrendered Expectation

With open hearts, we lay it down,
The weight of dreams, the thorns, the crown.
In silent trust, we find our peace,
From burdens heavy, we seek release.

Each moment held, a gift sublime,
In surrender's grace, we halt the time.
With faith we stand, in stillness true,
In every loss, a path anew.

Through trials faced, we learn to let,
The longing fade, our hearts inset.
In every hope, we whisper still,
For love will guide, for love will fill.

With gentle hands, we craft our fate,
In patience learned, we contemplate.
For in surrender, blooms the light,
That leads us on through darkest night.

So let us breathe, and trust the plan,
In every heart, His love will span.
Surrendered souls, forever bound,
In expectation's grace, we are found.

A Heart Never Forsaken

In shadows deep, a light will shine,
A whisper soft, a hand divine.
Though storms may rage, the heart stays true,
A love unbound, forever new.

When trials come, and hopes seem lost,
In faith we rise, despite the cost.
For in each break, the spirit grows,
A garden blooms from winter's throes.

The world may wane, like evening skies,
Yet in our hearts, eternal ties.
With every tear that falls like rain,
Is proof of joy that masks our pain.

In prayers we find our strength renewed,
In sacred bonds, our spirits glued.
A heart that trusts, shall never stray,
In love's embrace, we find our way.

So when you feel the dark descend,
Remember still, there is no end.
For in His grace, we are embraced,
A heart once lost, now found in grace.

Tethered by Love

In every breath, love's tether stays,
A link divine, through all our days.
In quiet moments, hearts align,
Together bound, by will divine.

When sorrow strikes and shadows call,
Love lifts us high, we shall not fall.
With every trial, a bond grows strong,
In sacred trust, we all belong.

Through laughter bright, and tears of grace,
Each heartbeat sings, love's sweet embrace.
In gentle whispers, souls unite,
Through darkest nights, we seek the light.

As seasons change and rivers flow,
Through peaks and valleys, love will show.
Each challenge met, with hands entwined,
In faith we walk, our hearts aligned.

So let us stand, forever bold,
In love's warm arms, a story told.
With every step, our spirits rise,
Tethered by love, we touch the skies.

Spiritual Embrace

In silent prayer, we find our way,
A sacred space, where shadows play.
In every heartbeat, spirits meet,
In love we walk, on holy street.

The gentle breeze whispers our names,
In every moment, love's sweet flames.
We gather strength from life divine,
In grace we stand, together shine.

With open hearts, we share our truth,
A journey blessed, enriched with youth.
In every touch, a spark ignites,
In harmony, our hope ignites.

As stars align and heavens gleam,
In faith we trust, in love we dream.
Through trials faced, our spirits soar,
In sacred bonds, we seek for more.

So let us rise, in joyful song,
In every heartbeat, we belong.
With open arms, we greet the night,
In spiritual embrace, we find our light.

The Pilgrim's Hold

With weary feet, the path unfolds,
A journey rich with stories told.
In every step, the heart will race,
A pilgrim's hold, in truth and grace.

Through winding roads and mountains high,
In quiet woods, beneath the sky.
With every dawn, new hope ignites,
In every heart, the spirit fights.

Where kindness dwells and faith prevails,
Through love's sweet song, the spirit sails.
In sacred places, souls we find,
As hands unite, our hearts entwined.

The journey long, yet spirits bold,
In every moment, love unfolds.
With every prayer, our souls shall rise,
In steadfast grace, we touch the skies.

So let us walk, with purpose clear,
In every challenge, hold thee near.
For in this quest, our hearts will grow,
A pilgrim's hold, forever flow.

Ties of the Spirit

In the stillness, hearts align,
Souls entwined through space and time.
Each whisper carries sacred grace,
Binding us in love's embrace.

Beneath the stars, our spirits soar,
In every prayer, we seek for more.
The light that shines within your eyes,
Reflects the truth, divinely wise.

Through trials faced, and joys we find,
The ties of spirit, intertwined.
With every breath, a vow renewed,
A path of faith, in solitude.

In shadows cast, we walk as one,
The journey shared, though battles won.
Through every tear, and every song,
Together, we are ever strong.

With open hearts, we share our gifts,
In loving kindness, our spirit lifts.
For in this bond, we come to see,
The endless grace of unity.

Devotion's Embers

From the ashes, fire glows,
In silent night, devotion grows.
A flicker bright in darkest hours,
The source of life, the heart's true powers.

Each prayer we raise, a spark ignites,
In humble hearts, our souls take flight.
With hands held high, we seek the light,
In every moment, love ignites.

Through trials faced and storms endured,
In faith we stand, forever assured.
Devotion's ember never fades,
In warmth and light, our path is laid.

With every dawn, renewed we rise,
In gratitude, we touch the skies.
Each step we take, a dance of grace,
In devotion's flame, we find our place.

The sacred bond we hold so dear,
In whispered hopes, our guides appear.
Together bound, our spirits shine,
In devotion's heat, we're intertwined.

The Sanctuary of Memory

In still reflection, shadows play,
Whispers of the past lead the way.
A sanctuary, heart's abode,
Where love's embraced, life gently flowed.

Each cherished moment, softly sown,
In quiet corners, kindness grown.
Through laughter shared and tears released,
In memory's arms, our pain finds peace.

The echoes bind, a sacred thread,
In portraits framed, the lives we've led.
Within these walls, the truth ignites,
A bond of souls that time unites.

Through every story, we are found,
In sacred silence, love abounds.
The hearts we've known, forever stay,
As memories guide us on our way.

In twilight's glow, we hold them close,
In every pulse, their love engrossed.
The sanctuary where spirits dwell,
In memories forged, we cast our spell.

Invincible Threads

In woven paths of fate, we tread,
With every knot, a story spread.
Threads of courage, faith, and love,
Binding us to forces above.

The tapestry of life unfolds,
In vibrant hues, our dreams are told.
Each silver strand a lesson learned,
In flickering flames, our hearts have burned.

Through trials faced and sorrows known,
The threads of hope are brightly sewn.
As hands unite in joyful grace,
Together we will find our place.

With every stitch, we rise anew,
In gratitude, we walk this view.
The invincible threads of our soul's weave,
In love embraced, we believe.

With faith in heart, we shall endure,
For in these ties, we are made sure.
Together bound, through storm and strife,
The threads of spirit shape our life.

The Spirit's Gentle Grasp

In quiet whispers, souls take flight,
The Spirit's grace, our guiding light.
With tender hands, it leads us near,
Embracing hearts, dispelling fear.

Each dawn reveals a sacred quest,
In every trial, we find our rest.
The gentle pull, a force divine,
In every heartbeat, love does shine.

Through valleys deep and mountains high,
The Spirit's breath, a soothing sigh.
In every moment, sacred ties,
A sacred bond that never dies.

When shadows loom and doubts arise,
The Spirit's song will neutralize.
In every tear, a joy unveiled,
With faith, our ship will never sail.

Embrace the touch, so soft and warm,
The Spirit's grasp, our sacred balm.
In unity, together we rise,
Toward the light beyond the skies.

Sturdy Roots of Belief

Though storms may rage and winds may blow,
In sturdy roots, our faith will grow.
Through trials faced, we stand up tall,
On ancient truths, we never fall.

With every seed of hope we plant,
In fertile ground, our hearts enchant.
The faith within us shines so bright,
Our sturdy roots in darkest night.

Through sacred texts and prayers profound,
We gather strength from hallowed ground.
With every chapter, every line,
Our spirits mix, like vintage wine.

When doubts arise, and shadows creep,
In sturdy roots, our promises keep.
A testament of love and grace,
In every challenge, we find place.

So let us stand, united, strong,
In sturdy roots, where we belong.
With every breath, our spirits soar,
In faith and love, forevermore.

The Veil of Hope's Embrace

In twilight's glow, where dreams reside,
The veil of hope, our faithful guide.
With each new dawn, the promise grows,
A gentle touch that ever flows.

Through darkest nights, the stars will shine,
Woven threads of fate, divine.
In every heart, a flicker glows,
The veil of hope, it softly shows.

In trials faced, we find our way,
The veil of hope will gently sway.
With open hands, we reach to trust,
In sacred bonds, we rise from dust.

When burdens weigh, and spirits tire,
The veil of hope ignites the fire.
A tender warmth, a sweet embrace,
Within each soul, a sacred space.

So let us walk in faith and grace,
Beneath the veil of hope's embrace.
In every heart and whispered prayer,
The veil of hope will always care.

Clinging to the Celestial Tide

In waves of grace, we find our way,
Clinging to love, come what may.
The celestial tide, both fierce and kind,
In every ebb, our hearts aligned.

With every rise, a chance to soar,
In unity, we seek for more.
Together bound by faith's embrace,
The celestial tide holds sacred space.

When tempests roar and dark winds blow,
We cling to faith, as rivers flow.
In every trial, we find the light,
In sacred waves, our souls take flight.

In quiet moments, we feel the pull,
The celestial tide, forever full.
Through every journey, every ride,
With steadfast hearts, we turn the tide.

So let us drift on love's own sea,
Clinging to the tide of sanctity.
In faith, we wade where waters glide,
Together, we embrace the celestial tide.

The Essential Anchors of Existence

In the stillness, faith takes flight,
Guiding hearts through darkest night.
Love's embrace, a sturdy dock,
In swirling tides, we stand and rock.

Hope's bright whisper lights the way,
Through trials faced, we choose to stay.
Compassion binds us, hand in hand,
A sacred thread, a promised land.

In unity, our voices rise,
Gentle echoes of the skies.
With every breath, we seek the truth,
A shared journey, ageless youth.

Forgiveness flows like rivers deep,
Restoring bonds that time may sweep.
With open hearts, we learn to heal,
In life's tapestry, love is real.

Gratitude transforms each day,
Finding joy in every way.
These anchors hold, through ebb and flow,
With faith and love, our spirits grow.

A Symphony of Grateful Souls

In morning's light, our voices blend,
A melody that knows no end.
With grateful hearts, we sing as one,
In every note, the light of sun.

Each moment shared, a dance divine,
In laughter's joy, our spirits shine.
Together bound, we rise anew,
In harmony, the old and true.

Through trials faced, we stand in grace,
With open arms, we find our place.
In whispered prayers, we seek the call,
A symphony that binds us all.

With every tear, a lesson learned,
In kindness shared, our hearts discerned.
In gratitude, our spirits soar,
We're woven close, forevermore.

In twilight's glow, we hold the light,
A chorus bright against the night.
With every breath, our praise we raise,
A symphony of endless days.

Wings of Refuge and Rest

Beneath the shade of love's embrace,
We find our peace, a sacred space.
In silence deep, our spirits blend,
With gentle wings, the heart can mend.

In trials faced, we seek the way,
A refuge where our worries lay.
With whispered prayers upon the breeze,
We find the strength that grants us ease.

Each moment held, a gift divine,
In presence felt, our souls align.
Together, we can rise and fly,
On wings of hope that touch the sky.

In evening's glow, we gather near,
With open hearts, we cast our fear.
Through love's embrace, we're intertwined,
A sanctuary, pure and kind.

In restful nights, our spirits rest,
In faith's embrace, we feel so blessed.
With each dawn, a promise starts,
Wings of refuge for our hearts.

The Fabric of Heavenly Kinship

In threads of love, we weave our ties,
A tapestry that never dies.
Each color shines with stories told,
In kinship warm, we find our gold.

Through laughter's thread and tears' embrace,
We stitch together every space.
In every heart, a piece we claim,
As woven souls, we share the same.

With every stitch, a sacred bond,
In life's great quilt, we wander on.
With open arms, we gather near,
In unity, we conquer fear.

The fabric strong, through storms we stand,
In love's own touch, we find our land.
Together here, we will remain,
In heavenly kinship, free from pain.

As stars align in night's embrace,
We shine together, face to face.
With gratitude, our hearts expand,
In this fabric, hand in hand.

Lanterns of Faith in the Night

In the shadowed paths we tread,
Lanterns glow with hope ahead,
Guiding hearts through darkest fears,
Illuminating silent prayers.

Held aloft by trusts that soar,
Each flicker opens heaven's door,
With every step, the light will swell,
For in our souls, His love will dwell.

O'er valleys deep and mountains grand,
Our faith, a compass in His hand,
Through storms that howl and tempests rage,
His lanterns shine, our hearts engage.

When doubt encroaches, shadows fall,
We rise together, answer the call,
For every candle, a vow to keep,
In the warmth of prayer, our spirits leap.

So let us walk, be never shy,
With faith like lanterns, reaching high,
Through night's embrace, we shall ignite,
The dawn of hope, His guiding light.

Sanctified by the Grasp of Prayer

In quiet moments, hearts entwined,
A sacred bond is softly signed,
As prayers ascend on wings of grace,
In every whisper, we find His face.

Each uttered word, a gentle plea,
A chance to nurture faith's decree,
Through trials faced and burdens borne,
In prayer's embrace, new strength is born.

Beneath the weight of endless night,
Our voices rise, a chorus bright,
In sacred silence, find the way,
Sanctified by the grasp of prayer.

We gather close in trust divine,
In unity, our hearts align,
With every prayer, the heavens bend,
A path of light, in love we send.

O, crafters of hope, on knees we kneel,
Our souls laid bare, our truths reveal,
Through every sigh and joyful tear,
His presence lingers, ever near.

The Sweet Surrender of Trust

In the stillness, we release,
A gentle hush, a breath of peace,
With open arms, we yield to grace,
The sweet surrender, a warm embrace.

In trials faced and storms endured,
Our faith in Him, forever assured,
Through every doubt, through every fear,
Trust plants its roots; His love draws near.

With hearts aligned, we learn to wait,
For grace bestowed will not be late,
The sweet surrender teaches us,
In His great plan, we place our trust.

Each moment lived, a step divine,
In surrender, our spirits shine,
For He who guides, will lead the way,
In sweet surrender, we shall stay.

So let us walk, hand in hand with fate,
Embracing love that resonates,
For in His light, our burdens rust,
In quiet hearts, the gift of trust.

Echoes of Eternal Embrace

In every heartbeat, echoed grace,
The whispers of a warm embrace,
Through time and trials, love remains,
In sacred silence, joy attains.

With arms outstretched, we find our way,
In every night, there's hope for day,
As echoes ring through ancient skies,
His love, a lantern, never dies.

In every laugh, in every tear,
Eternal love is always near,
In every moment spent in prayer,
We find the solace, He will share.

For every wound and every scar,
An echo calls, no distance far,
In every soul, the light ignites,
An eternal dance of sacred rights.

So let us breathe in unity,
In echo's grace, we'll always be,
For in His arms, all fears erase,
In echoes sweet, our hearts embrace.

Through Storms of the Soul

In tempest's grip, we find our fight,
Faith whispers softly, guiding light.
Each wave that crashes, a lesson taught,
Through storms of anguish, peace is sought.

The heart endures, through pain it grows,
In trials faced, true strength it shows.
With every raindrop, a tear to shed,
Hope blooms anew, where fear once led.

We seek His grace amidst the plight,
In darkest hours, His hand ignites.
Though winds may howl, we stand our ground,
In sacred trust, our souls are bound.

From clouds that thunder, His voice we hear,
In sacred silence, He draws us near.
Through raging storms, we walk with pride,
With hearts anchored deep, in Him we bide.

Emerging strong from stormy seas,
Our spirits rise, with gentle ease.
The sun will shine when shadows fade,
In every trial, His love displayed.

Hearts Resilient in Prayer

In quiet corners, voices rise,
Hearts entwined, beneath the skies.
With every whisper, a bond is spun,
In prayer's embrace, our souls are one.

Through fervent pleas, our spirits soar,
With gratitude, we seek for more.
Each word a candle, casting light,
In night's deep shadows, hope ignites.

We gather strength, when trials press,
In faith's foundation, we find rest.
With every tear, a blessing flows,
Our hearts resilient, love bestows.

In moments of doubt, we reach for grace,
Within His arms, we find our place.
Each prayer a journey, paths unfold,
In sacred trust, our stories told.

Together we rise, united in care,
In hearts resilient, we lay bare.
As light breaks through, our spirits gleam,
In prayer, forever, we are redeemed.

The Compass of Devoted Souls

In silent nights, the stars align,
Guiding our hearts, through dark's design.
With faith as compass, we chart our way,
In devotion's light, we find our sway.

Through winding paths, the journey's long,
In every struggle, we find our song.
Each step we take, in spirit we trust,
In shared devotion, our hearts combust.

The map of love, our sacred guide,
Where hope and mercy gently reside.
A beacon gleams, in shadows cast,
With every heartbeat, our ties hold fast.

In moments of doubt, we listen close,
For in His whispers, our spirits coalesce.
Through storms and trials, we find our role,
Ever united, devoted souls.

As dawn breaks forth, we see the way,
In peace and grace, we start the day.
Together we strive, in love we stand,
With faith as compass, hand in hand.

Shadows and Light: The Sacred Balance

In depths of night, shadows may creep,
Yet in the dark, promises keep.
With every doubt that taints the soul,
Hope dances softly, making us whole.

The sun will rise on weary hearts,
In light's embrace, our fear departs.
For every shadow that looms ahead,
A beam of grace will be our thread.

Life's ebb and flow, a sacred dance,
In joy and sorrow, we find our chance.
Each moment teaches, each lesson learned,
In balance found, our spirits yearned.

In stormy skies, we seek His face,
From shadows deep, emerges grace.
We journey forth, with faith as guide,
In love's embrace, we shall abide.

Through every trial, the light shines bright,
In sacred balance, we find our might.
Together we walk, through day and night,
In shadows and light, our hearts ignite.

A Well of Faith

In the quiet heart, a whisper flows,
A well of grace, where hope still grows.
Beneath the stars, in twilight's glow,
We gather strength, in love we know.

With each small drop, the spirit's calm,
In trials faced, we find the balm.
A gentle touch, a sacred guide,
Through darkened paths, we will abide.

From depths unseen, the power springs,
In every prayer, the soul still sings.
A fortress built on faith and trust,
In every heart, a holy gust.

Together strong, we walk the way,
With light divine, we greet the day.
In unity, our voices rise,
To meet the heavens, where love ties.

For in this well, we find our peace,
In every heart, may joy increase.
Through whispered prayers, we find our place,
In the embrace of boundless grace.

Embracing the Infinite

Open your heart, to skies so wide,
Where love abounds, and fears subside.
In every breath, let grace unfold,
Embrace the light, both warm and bold.

Stars in the night, they softly gleam,
A tapestry of hope, we dream.
In every moment, the sacred calls,
In loving arms, the spirit sprawls.

Infinite fields of love do grace,
In every soul, a shining face.
In unity, we find our worth,
A homage deep, to our shared birth.

With faith as anchor, we will soar,
Beyond the shadows, to evermore.
In journeys bold, we walk with trust,
For in His path, we rise from dust.

Embracing all, both near and far,
In timeless love, we find the star.
In every heartbeat, joy shall sing,
In the infinite, our lives take wing.

Graceful Grips of Faith

With open hands, we clasp the light,
In every prayer, we find our sight.
In struggles faced, our hearts unite,
For in His grace, we find our might.

Each gentle touch, a sacred bond,
Through trials faced, our spirits respond.
In whispered hopes, the soul takes flight,
With every tear, we seek the right.

Moments small, yet vast in reach,
With love and trust, the lessons teach.
Through valleys deep, we learn to stand,
In faithful hugs, we clasp His hand.

Together we rise, in faith we walk,
In every breath, we start to talk.
In grace's grip, our sorrows fade,
For in His love, a joy is laid.

So let us hold, the light so near,
With every pulse, dispel the fear.
In graceful grips, we find our way,
In faith's embrace, we greet the day.

Beneath the Weight of Prayer

In silence deep, our spirits sigh,
Beneath the weight, our hearts comply.
With every thought, a prayer ascends,
In trusting hands, our spirit bends.

Through burdens felt, we lift our gaze,
In trembling faith, we seek His ways.
Each whispered word, a sacred vow,
In quiet moments, we humbly bow.

As dawn arises, hope ignites,
With every prayer, the heart unites.
In shadows cast, our faith will shine,
In every struggle, love divine.

Beneath the weight, we find our strength,
In every journey, love at length.
Through trials faced, our spirits soar,
With open hearts, we seek for more.

In glorious light, we find our peace,
With thankful hearts, our fears release.
Beneath the weight of prayer, we rise,
In holy grace, we touch the skies.

In the Depths of Devotion

In quiet spaces, hearts entwine,
With every prayer, a sacred sign.
The light within, a guiding flame,
In humble whispers, call His name.

Through trials faced, our spirits rise,
In faith, we seek the holy skies.
His love abounds, a gentle stream,
In devotion's depth, we find our dream.

A path of grace, where hope is sown,
In every moment, we are known.
With open arms, He welcomes all,
In pure devotion, we shall stand tall.

With every breath, we offer praise,
In sacred rituals, lift our gaze.
In silent reverie, peace will bloom,
In the depths of love, dispel all gloom.

The Unseen Embrace of Trust

In shadows deep, our faith takes flight,
With every doubt, we seek the Light.
An unseen force, a gentle guide,
In trust, we find our hearts abide.

Through storms that rage, we anchor fast,
In every trial, there's grace amassed.
With every tear, a lesson learned,
In trust unfurled, our souls are turned.

In whispers soft, His promise speaks,
In darkest nights, it's Him we seek.
With open hearts, we rise anew,
In trust, we find our path so true.

With courage bold, we take each step,
In faith's embrace, the soul is kept.
In every heartbeat, love prevails,
In unseen trust, our spirit sails.

Chains of Reverent Love

Bound by grace, our spirits sing,
In love's embrace, we find our wing.
With gentle hands, we break the chain,
In reverence, our hearts remain.

Each act we hold, a sacred bond,
In unity, our voices respond.
With fervent hearts, we share the load,
In chains of love, we find our road.

When trials beckon, we hold fast,
In love's embrace, our fears are cast.
In every heartbeat, sweet and pure,
In reverent love, our souls endure.

Together we tread, a sacred path,
In light of faith, we find our math.
Bound as one, in service bright,
In chains of love, we spread the light.

Holding Fast to Heaven's Whisper

In silence deep, we heed His call,
With earnest hearts, we seek for all.
A whispered truth, in stillness found,
Holding fast, our souls are bound.

With open ears, we hear the grace,
In every moment, His warm embrace.
With faith like wings, we soar above,
In Heaven's whisper, we find love.

Through trials faced, we find our way,
In storms of life, He'll never sway.
With every word, a promise clear,
Holding fast to love, we'll persevere.

In sacred light, our paths align,
With every heartbeat, love divine.
In trust we stand, not lost, but near,
Holding fast to whispers dear.

Faithful Grasp

In shadows deep, we place our trust,
With every breath, our spirits adjust.
Through trials fierce, our hearts will soar,
In faith we find, forevermore.

A guiding light through darkest night,
We stand as one, our souls ignite.
With faithful grasp, we rise anew,
In love divine, we'll see us through.

Each whispered prayer, a sacred thread,
We honor paths the ancients tread.
With hands held high, we seek the way,
In unity, we choose to stay.

Through storms we sail, our hearts entwined,
In every loss, new strength we find.
For in our struggle, grace abides,
With every fall, our hope still rides.

So let us walk this journey bold,
With faith as strong, our story told.
Together bound, we face the dawn,
In faithful grasp, we journey on.

The Ties That Bind

In whispered vows and sacred ties,
In every gaze, love never lies.
Through trials faced and storms weathered,
The ties that bind, forever tethered.

In laughter shared and tears that flow,
In heartbeats fast, the truth will show.
With every heartbeat, hopes entwined,
Through darkest nights, love's light we find.

Each step is grace, each moment blessed,
In every test, we seek the best.
With hands held tight, we chase the dream,
For in His light, we are a team.

In faith we stand, through thick and thin,
No loss too great, no way too grim.
Our spirits joined, we dare to climb,
The ties that bind, through space and time.

So let our hearts in love reside,
In every moment, side by side.
The ties we share, a sacred bond,
A journey taken, of which we're fond.

Clinging to the Light

In weary nights when hope seems lost,
We gather strength, regardless of cost.
With open hearts, we seek the flame,
Clinging to the light, His holy name.

With every prayer, a gentle spark,
In love's embrace, we find the arc.
Through every storm, through every fight,
We hold to faith, we cling to light.

A beacon bright that shows the way,
In darkest hours, we choose to stay.
For in His warmth, our fears take flight,
Together strong, we cling to light.

With hands uplifted, spirits bold,
In every story, His love unfolds.
With voices raised, we sing His praise,
Clinging to the light, in endless days.

So let us shine, let hope ignite,
Through every trial, grasping tight.
For in His grace, we find our might,
Together forever, clinging to light.

Anchored in Grace

In raging seas, we cast our plea,
With gentle hands, He covers me.
Through trials fierce, we find our place,
In every moment, anchored in grace.

With every wave, His love remains,
Through all our joy, through all our pains.
In still of night, we seek His face,
Firm in Our hearts, anchored in grace.

Through tempests wild, our hearts do soar,
In faith we trust, forevermore.
With every breath, He leads the way,
Our compass sure, come what may.

In sacred bond, our spirits rise,
We find our truth in His wise eyes.
With hope alive, we run the race,
Together strong, anchored in grace.

So let us walk, with hearts aligned,
In every challenge, love defined.
For in His arms, we find our space,
In every moment, anchored in grace.

Arms Open to the Infinite

In stillness, hearts align with grace,
Each breath a prayer, each moment a chase.
With eyes uplifted to the heavenly light,
We gather hope in the calm of night.

The stars remind of promises made,
In the vast expanse, never to fade.
Love transcends the bounds of fate,
In the arms of the Infinite, we wait.

Every whisper sings of a sacred bond,
In the depths of silence, souls respond.
With open arms, we greet the dawn,
Guided by faith, forever drawn.

Through trials and storms, we stand as one,
In the presence of mercy, we've just begun.
Each tear of sorrow a seed to grow,
In the garden of love, abundance flows.

With radiant light, the path is clear,
In every heartbeat, we feel you near.
Together we journey, hearts intertwined,
In the arms of the Infinite, truth we find.

The Unbreakable Covenant of Care

In the quiet moments, love takes its stand,
A solemn promise, hand in hand.
Through trials that test, we rise above,
Bound by the unbreakable covenant of love.

In joy and sorrow, we share the weight,
Every smile a blessing, every tear fate.
Through valleys low and mountains high,
We weave our lives under the sacred sky.

Compassion's flame burns bright and clear,
In the heart's embrace, we hold each dear.
With gentle whispers and steadfast grace,
In every moment, we find our place.

Together we rise, as one we stand,
In the tapestry of life, a divine strand.
With faith as our anchor, we journey far,
Guided by love, our guiding star.

For in every heartbeat, a story unfolds,
Of kindness and hope that never grows old.
In the unbreakable covenant we share,
Eternally bound, in the light we care.

In the Shadow of the Divine

In the stillness of night, where whispers flow,
We find our refuge in the sacred glow.
In the shadow of the Divine, we retreat,
Where love surrounds and hearts meet.

With every heartbeat, a sacred hymn,
In the silence, we let the light begin.
Guided by faith through the darkest hour,
In the embrace of grace, we find our power.

Each tear a testament, each laugh a song,
In the shadow of the Divine, we belong.
With every step on this holy ground,
In the depths of peace, our souls are found.

Together we wander, unafraid to seek,
In the bounty of love, we hear you speak.
With hands uplifted, we touch the sky,
In the shadow of the Divine, we fly.

For here we find hope, and endless light,
In the warmth of the Divine, everything's right.
With hearts ablaze in the endless grace,
In the shadow of the Divine, we embrace.

Faith's Resilient Touch

In storms of doubt, we lean on light,
Through every struggle, faith takes flight.
With resilient hearts, we rise anew,
In faith's gentle touch, hope breaks through.

Each trial faced, a lesson learned,
In the fires of life, our spirits burned.
With every challenge, faith grows strong,
In unity and love, we all belong.

Through whispers of grace that speak our name,
In the tapestry of time, we forge our flame.
With open hearts and eyes that see,
In faith's resilient touch, we are free.

Together we stand on this sacred ground,
With arms outstretched, in love we're found.
Through the seasons of life, our souls entwine,
In faith's embrace, our paths align.

So let us walk with courage and trust,
In the journey of life, in love we must.
With faith's resilient touch, we shall soar,
In the arms of grace, forevermore.

Bonds Forged in the Flame of Love

In the heart's deep chamber, love does sing,
A flame ignites, a sacred offering.
Together we rise, as shadows fade,
In this bond of grace, our fears dismade.

With hands entwined, we tread this path,
Through trials faced, we find our wrath.
For love, a force that stirs the soul,
In its warm embrace, we become whole.

A sacred fire, unyielding and true,
In every heartbeat, I am with you.
Through whispered prayers and silent nights,
Our spirits soar, like heavenly kites.

In the depths of sorrow, joy shall bloom,
Together we dance, dispelling gloom.
Each moment shared, a testament bold,
In love's embrace, our stories told.

Through trials long, our bond shall shine,
In the flame of love, a gift divine.
Hand in hand, we rise above,
For all is well, when we're in love.

In the Gentle Cradle of the Divine

In a cradle soft, where shadows fade,
The gentle hand of grace is laid.
With whispers sweet, the Spirit calls,
In every breath, the love enfalls.

The morning light, a promise new,
In every dawn, we feel it too.
The heart beats strong, in sacred trust,
In this divine cradle, we adjust.

As rivers flow, and seasons change,
The love we nurture, nothing strange.
In laughter shared, and tears we weep,
The gentle cradle, our souls to keep.

With every star, a prayer we send,
In the divine embrace, our hearts mend.
In silence found, we hear the call,
In the gentle cradle, love conquers all.

So let us rise, to greet the day,
In faith and love, we find our way.
Together we stand, our spirits shine,
In the gentle cradle, your heart in mine.

Time's Unfurling Tapestry

In the loom of life, we weave our thread,
Each moment a stitch, where hopes are spread.
With colors bright, and shadows cast,
We find our strength in the present vast.

The hands of time, they gently guide,
Through every tear, love's light abide.
In every fold, our stories blend,
A tapestry rich, with threads we send.

With every heartbeat, time unfolds,
A sacred tale, in whispers told.
In laughter shared, in silence sought,
The fabric of life, with love is wrought.

Through valleys low and mountains high,
In faith we journey, beneath the sky.
With each new dawn, new patterns arise,
In time's embrace, our spirits rise.

So let us weave with hearts sincere,
In the tapestry of life, love is near.
Together we'll stitch, with threads of gold,
In time's unfurling, our hearts unfold.

The Radiance of Shared Belief

In unity's glow, our vision clear,
Together we stand, casting off fear.
With hopes ablaze, our spirits take flight,
In shared belief, we find our light.

Each voice in chorus, harmony sings,
In faith's embrace, our souls take wings.
In the depths of prayer, we find our place,
Guided by love, and boundless grace.

For as we gather, the light will grow,
In every heart, the truth we know.
With every step, together we tread,
In the radiance of love, we are led.

Through trials faced and storms endured,
In shared belief, we are assured.
With courage fierce, our spirits soar,
Together we rise, forevermore.

So let us stand, with hands held tight,
In the warmth of faith, we find our might.
For in the bonds of shared belief,
We carry forth the sweet relief.

A Dance of Loving Kindness

In grace we gather, hand in hand,
With gentle whispers, we understand.
Each heart a vessel, love's embrace,
In every moment, we seek Your face.

Beneath the heavens, we twirl and sway,
In joyful cadence, we find our way.
With every step, the light unfolds,
A dance of kindness, as love beholds.

Together we rise, as one we sing,
Joy in our souls, His praises bring.
In harmony's truth, we lift our voice,
In His embrace, we all rejoice.

Through trials faced, we never part,
With tender strength, we guard our heart.
In every shadow, His love's the key,
In a dance of kindness, we are free.

The Woven Garment of Salvation

Threads of mercy, spun divine,
Intertwined in love's design.
With every stitch, our hope is sewn,
A garment bright, our spirits grown.

From sorrow's loom, to joy's embrace,
In woven patterns, we find our place.
A cloak of faith, so richly worn,
In trials faced, we are reborn.

When darkness falls, the light appears,
Guiding us through our darkest fears.
Each strand a promise, every hue,
In salvation's fabric, we are new.

Let hearts unite, in love we stand,
Together weaving, hand in hand.
In the Savior's grace, our burdens cease,
In the woven garment, we find peace.

Melodies of Hopeful Hearts

In quiet moments, our spirits rise,
With songs of hope that reach the skies.
Each note a prayer, each chord a grace,
In melody sweet, we seek Your face.

In trials faced, the music plays,
The heartbeats echo love's embrace.
With every rhythm, a bridge is made,
Connecting souls, never to fade.

In joyful harmonies, we proclaim,
His love unchanging, always the same.
Through valleys deep, we find the way,
With melodies bright, we choose to stay.

Let hope resound in every heart,
A symphony where love won't part.
For in the music, we clearly see,
The gift of faith, He gives us free.

Threads of Unwavering Light

In the fabric of life, light we weave,
Through trials and storms, we believe.
With every thread, His love we find,
A tapestry rich, by grace designed.

Unbroken strands, from darkness to dawn,
Guiding us gently, a path reborn.
In every challenge, strength we gain,
With threads of light, we break the chain.

Through shadows cast, our spirits soar,
In unwavering truth, we seek no more.
The light that shines in every heart,
A guiding star, we'll never part.

Together we stand, with love as our guide,
In a world of hope, we will abide.
With threads of light, forever bright,
In His embrace, we find our sight.

The Covenant of Souls

In quiet whispers, hearts entwine,
A promise forged in love divine.
Together we walk the sacred path,
Guided by faith in the aftermath.

Through trials faced, our spirits soar,
In unity, we find the door.
To realms where truth and grace abide,
In harmony, we now confide.

With every breath, a prayer we raise,
In gratitude, we sing our praise.
For every soul carries the flame,
In His name, we are never the same.

Let bonds of love remind us still,
Each covenant meets Heaven's will.
In sacred trust, we shall remain,
Through joy and sorrow, through loss and gain.

For in the covenant of our hearts,
The light of God forever starts.
A tapestry of souls in light,
We stand united, bold, and bright.

Serenity in Surrender

In stillness found, the spirit bends,
A heart that breaks for love transcends.
In quiet waters, peace does flow,
In whispered faith, we let it go.

With hands held high, we seek the grace,
In every tear, we find our place.
For in the night, the dawn will rise,
In humble prayer, our spirits fly.

The world may roar, but here we stand,
Embraced by faith, guided by hand.
In surrender, we find our light,
A beacon shining through the night.

Let worries fade like morning mist,
In every moment, we persist.
For in the arms of love divine,
We breathe the calm of His design.

Serenity blooms in hearts that yield,
In every trial, strength revealed.
So let us journey, hand in hand,
In trusting love, together we stand.

Transcending the Tempest

When storms arise and shadows loom,
Our faith shall guide us through the gloom.
In raging winds, our spirits soar,
For love prevails and opens doors.

Through every trial, we shall find,
The light that leads and breaks the blind.
With courage firm, we stand our ground,
In faith and hope, our strength is found.

The tempest roars, yet hearts remain,
In trust, we dance amidst the rain.
For every wave that seeks to drown,
A steadfast love shall wear the crown.

With open hearts, we rise once more,
From depths of pain, the spirit soars.
Transcend the storm, embrace the trial,
In every moment, we find our smile.

For in the storm, the calm we seek,
A whispered truth, both loud and meek.
A voice that guides us through the night,
In tempest's wake, we find the light.

A Touch Beyond Time

In every heartbeat, love resides,
A sacred bond that never hides.
Beyond the veil of space and year,
A touch of grace, forever near.

In timelessness, our souls entwine,
In glances shared, a love divine.
For every moment, fleeting yet bright,
We dwell in shadows, kissed by light.

Through endless ages, a thread remains,
In whispers soft, love breaks the chains.
A dance of souls, forever spun,
In unity, our hearts are one.

Each touch transcends the sands of time,
In fervent vows, our spirits climb.
For love that lingers, never fades,
In sacred silence, truth cascades.

In every story, love's refrain,
A touch beyond, in joy and pain.
Eternal echoes, freely given,
In every heart, our love is risen.

The Warmth of Belief

In the dawn of hope we rise,
Hearts ignited by the skies,
With each prayer, a gentle light,
Guiding souls through the night.

Faith, a flame within the heart,
With every whisper, we depart,
From shadows dark, to paths so bright,
Together walking toward the light.

With hands united, strong and true,
In love and trust, we will renew,
Each moment shared, a sacred sign,
Our spirits soar, forever entwined.

Through trials faced, we stand as one,
In every battle, battles won,
For in our core, the truth we hold,
A story of love, forever told.

The warmth of belief, a guiding flame,
In every heart, it speaks our name,
A bond of joy that none can sever,
Together in faith, now and forever.

In the Embrace of Grace

In quiet moments, grace descends,
A gentle whisper, it transcends,
With open hearts, we seek to find,
The love that binds, the ties that bind.

In every challenge, there's a way,
To rise anew with each new day,
For burdens shared make spirits light,
In the embrace of love's pure light.

Through valleys low and mountains high,
We find our strength, we spread our wings,
In humble praise, we learn to sing,
Together in joy, forever rings.

Awash in grace, our fears release,
In every moment, find our peace,
Through trials faced, we stand as one,
In grateful hearts, our race is run.

In the embrace of grace divine,
Our spirits lift, our souls align,
With faith unbroken, we shall soar,
In love eternal, forevermore.

Visions of Faith

In the stillness of the night,
Visions blossom, clear and bright,
Stars above, like wishes cast,
Guide us home, our doubts surpassed.

Through every trial, every tear,
The voice of faith, so strong, so near,
A beacon shone, in darkest hours,
Reminding us of hidden powers.

With open hearts, we seek the way,
In whispered prayers, we softly say,
That love can heal, and hope can save,
In dreams of faith, we find our brave.

From pain and loss, new life will bloom,
In every shadow, light will loom,
For faith ignites our inner fire,
A sacred song, our souls' desire.

Visions of faith, a precious gift,
In every moment, hearts will lift,
Together we stand, in trust and grace,
Forever bound, in love's embrace.

Strength in Reverence

In quiet reverence, we bow low,
A sacred moment, the soul's glow,
With every heartbeat, we connect,
In faith, our hearts, we do protect.

Through storms that rage, we hold our ground,
In strength of spirit, peace is found,
For every challenge that we face,
We rise anew with boundless grace.

In gentle whispers, we unite,
With open hearts, we seek the light,
Each prayer a thread, a bond so strong,
In reverence, where we belong.

With hands outstretched, we seek and find,
The strength within, the ties that bind,
Through every trial, we will stand,
In reverence, hand in hand.

Strength in reverence, vast and wide,
In faith, we take this sacred ride,
Together in love, we find our way,
Strengthened in trust, come what may.

Embracing the Divine

In quiet prayer, I seek Your face,
A gentle heart, in sacred space.
Your love surrounds, like morning light,
Guiding my soul through darkest night.

With every breath, I whisper peace,
In troubled times, my doubts release.
Your grace, a river, flows so wide,
In You, my Spirit shall abide.

When burdens rise, and tempests roar,
Your hand is strong, forevermore.
I find my strength in Your embrace,
The world transformed, in love's warm grace.

Each step I take, with faith in heart,
I walk this path, though torn apart.
In trials deep, I trust Your will,
Embracing all, my heart is still.

The Unyielding Embrace

In shadows cast, Your light remains,
Through weary roads, through endless pains.
Your arms, a fortress, strong and wide,
In You, dear Lord, I will abide.

As storms may howl, and fears arise,
I lift my gaze to endless skies.
Your love, a balm, for every soul,
In You, O God, I find my whole.

With each surrender, I am free,
In tender grace, You gather me.
Your whispers calm the restless waves,
In faith, I trust; my heart now saves.

Though life may shake, and hope may wane,
Your steadfast love, my joyful gain.
Within Your heart, I find my base,
In truth, O Lord, I've found my grace.

Shadows of Hope

In shadows deep, where fears may dwell,
I seek Your light, O heart of swell.
Each whispered prayer, a spark ignites,
Your hope, my guide through darkest nights.

Through valleys low, Your voice I hear,
In pain and doubt, You draw me near.
With every tear, a promise made,
In every sorrow, love displayed.

The dawn shall break, a tender glow,
In every heart, a seed to sow.
Your faithfulness, like stars above,
In every loss, I feel Your love.

So onward still, with courage swell,
In shadows deep, I know You dwell.
My heart will sing in joyful praise,
For You, O Lord, my hope shall raise.

Beneath the Wings of Mercy

Beneath the wings of mercy wide,
I find my peace, my soul's true guide.
In trials faced, Your love my shield,
In every moment, I am healed.

Your gentle touch, a warm embrace,
In every storm, I find my place.
With every breath, I trust Your name,
In darkness found, I feel no shame.

The road ahead may twist and turn,
In every heart, a sacred yearn.
Your promises, like morning dew,
Refresh my spirit, ever true.

Each time I fall, Your grace will rise,
With faith in You, I touch the skies.
In boundless love, I tread this way,
Beneath Your wings, I long to stay.

Cherished Shadows

In the stillness of the night,
Soft whispers call our name,
Angels guide through darkest hours,
With love, they fan the flame.

Within the shadows stands a light,
A beacon strong and pure,
Faith leads the way through trials faced,
In hope, our hearts endure.

Each tear we shed, a prayer released,
Cleansing all our pain,
From sorrow blooms a fragrant grace,
In loss, there's still a gain.

Beneath the stars, our spirits rise,
The heavens hear our cries,
In cherished shadows, joy abides,
Where whispered love never dies.

Let every heart embrace the night,
And find the sacred glow,
For in the darkness, we are loved,
In shadows, faith will grow.

The Path of the Devout

Each step we take on hallowed ground,
Is blessed with grace divine,
With hearts aligned to heaven's chords,
Our spirits intertwine.

Through valleys deep and mountains high,
A journey fraught with hope,
In trials faced, we rise anew,
Our faith will help us cope.

Prayers whispered on the breeze,
Carry us with gentle hands,
Through life's storms and raging seas,
In love, the heart expands.

Compassion leads our every deed,
As kindness lights the way,
We serve the weary, mend the lost,
And turn night into day.

The path of the devout shall shine,
With each selfless embrace,
In unity, we walk in peace,
Together, we find grace.

Mirrored in the Soul

Within the depths of every heart,
Reflects the light of love,
A sacred bond that knows no bounds,
A gift from up above.

In silence, we can hear the call,
Of spirits intertwined,
A dance of faith, where we all share,
The poetry of the divine.

Beneath the stars, our souls unite,
In harmony we sing,
With every breath, the sacred breath,
To life, our hearts we bring.

Through trials passed, our lessons learned,
In faith, we find our way,
For every tear, a chance to grow,
With love that will not sway.

Mirrored in the soul's embrace,
Is where our spirits soar,
Together, hand in hand, we'll walk,
Towards forevermore.

Sacred Roots

In the earth, our roots run deep,
Anchored in sacred ground,
With every prayer, we nurture life,
In silence, love is found.

From ancient trees to blooming flowers,
The spirit brings us near,
A tapestry of faith and hope,
Woven through each tear.

In the seasons of our lives,
We face the sun and rain,
With every change, we grow and learn,
In strength, we find no pain.

Sacred are the bonds we share,
Lifetimes intertwined,
Beneath the stars, we whisper dreams,
In unity defined.

With roots that hold, we rise above,
In love, our souls take flight,
For in the heart of every prayer,
We find the purest light.

Bonds Beyond the Veil

In whispers soft, our spirits dance,
With cosmic ties, in a sacred trance.
Though bodies part, our souls unite,
In realms of love, we find the light.

Through shadows cast, our faith does bloom,
In every heart, dispelling gloom.
Eternal bonds that death can't sever,
In timeless grace, we dwell forever.

In prayerful hearts, connection grows,
As blessings flow like gentle prose.
United in spirit, we walk the way,
In heavenly peace, we choose to stay.

With every breath, we feel His call,
A promise kept, love conquers all.
Beyond the veil, we seek and find,
The sacred truth that binds mankind.

In stillness deep, we hear the song,
Of those we've loved, who still belong.
In Death's embrace, we shall not fear,
For love transcends, and draws us near.

Soaring on Spirit's Wings

With faith as wings, we rise above,
Embracing grace, and endless love.
In spirit's flight, we find our way,
To sacred realms, where night meets day.

In morning's light, our hearts refine,
A journey blessed, by His design.
With every step, the soul ascends,
In sacred trust, where joy transcends.

Through trials faced, we learn to soar,
In unity, we seek for more.
With every prayer, the spirit glows,
On wings of hope, our essence flows.

In whispered prayers, our spirits meet,
In holy silence, we feel Him sweet.
With open hearts, we soar the skies,
In love's embrace, our spirit flies.

With every heartbeat, we draw near,
To realms of grace, to hearts sincere.
In cherub's light, we rise and sing,
As one in faith, on spirit's wing.

Resilient in Reverence

In trials faced, our spirits stand,
With humble hearts, we hold His hand.
Through stormy nights, our faith holds true,
In reverent grace, we see anew.

With courage found in every fall,
We rise again, responding His call.
In sacred strength, we find our peace,
From pain and strife, our hearts release.

In gratitude, our voices soar,
To realms of light forevermore.
With hearts aflame, we praise His name,
In every struggle, we find our claim.

With every step, our souls arise,
In reverent awe, beneath the skies.
The path of grace, though steep and long,
In faith's embrace, we grow more strong.

In stillness deep, we find our way,
With faith beside us, come what may.
Resilient hearts in love we weave,
In sacred trust, we shall believe.

The Guardian's Light

In darkness deep, His light will shine,
A beacon bright, forever mine.
With every step, I know He's near,
Guiding my heart, dispelling fear.

Each whispered prayer, a soothing balm,
In turbulent seas, the soul finds calm.
With every trial, His love bestowed,
A guardian's light, upon the road.

Through valleys deep, His hand I hold,
In warmth of faith, my heart consoled.
With gentle whispers, He leads the way,
In shadows cast, my hope shall stay.

With every dawn, I feel His grace,
In every moment, I seek His face.
The guardian's watch upon my soul,
In sacred trust, I feel made whole.

In love's embrace, I walk in peace,
With every heartbeat, my fears release.
The light of the guardian shines so bright,
In faith's embrace, I find true light.

The Warmth of Intertwined Prayers

In sacred whispers, our hopes align,
Threads of devotion, in faith we entwine.
Hearts lifted high, like stars that we chase,
Together we seek the divine's warm embrace.

In the stillness of night, prayers softly rise,
Echoing softly, like murmured sighs.
Each voice a flicker, a candle's soft light,
Igniting the dark with a promise of night.

With hands held together, we stand side by side,
In storms and in sunlight, our spirits abide.
We gather as one, both humble and bold,
Our stories of faith in each other retold.

Each breath a blessing, a gift from above,
In laughter and tears, we feel His great love.
Through valleys of sorrow, through mountain's high peak,

In the warmth of our prayers, His comfort we seek.

So let us unite in this circle of grace,
Glimmers of hope in each tear-streaked face.
For the warmth of our prayers reaches far and wide,
In sacred communion, forever we bide.

The Crucible of Loving Resilience

Through trials and strife, our spirits are forged,
In the crucible's fire, our hearts are enlarged.
With love as our beacon, we rise without fear,
Together we flourish, with hands ever near.

Endurance in faith, like roots deep and strong,
We weather the storms; we right every wrong.
Each lesson a stone on our pathway to grace,
In the dance of resilience, we find our place.

With kindness our armor, we cherish the weak,
In the face of despair, it's hope that we seek.
Through ashes we blossom, in shadows we shine,
In unity's warmth, our spirits combine.

The journey is long, through valleys we roam,
Yet love is the compass that leads us back home.
Each tear that we shed is a testament sweet,
To the strength of our hearts, as we rise to defeat.

Embracing this journey, hand in hand we tread,
With faith as our guide, where angels have led.
In the crucible's light, our purpose we find,
Loving resilience, our hearts intertwined.

The Collective Heartbeat of Belief

In the quiet moments, our hearts beat as one,
Pulsing with rhythms, of grace we're spun.
Bound by our faith, in love we rely,
The collective heartbeat, a symphony high.

Each prayer a note in this sacred score,
When faith is our guide, we always find more.
Together in worship, our spirits take flight,
Illuminating darkness with courage and light.

From whispers of comfort to shouts of joy,
In the chorus of love, no soul is a toy.
In silence and song, we find our way home,
In the depth of our bond, we're never alone.

Through trials and triumphs, this melody flows,
In the tapestry woven, our belief ever grows.
Across every distance, through valleys we tread,
The heartbeat of belief always gently spreads.

So let us lift praises and let spirits soar,
With each beating heart, we'll always want more.
In the music of faith, together we thrive,
The collective heartbeat, forever alive.

Circles of Radiant Devotion

In circles of trust, where love finds its way,
We gather in spirit, to joyfully pray.
With hearts open wide, we share in the light,
Radiant devotion, a beautiful sight.

Each voice in the round, a harmonious sound,
In unity's bliss, together we're bound.
Through trials and triumphs, we stand as a whole,
In the circle of faith, we nurture the soul.

The warmth of connection, in laughter we find,
Each story a thread, in the fabric entwined.
With kindness and grace, we lift one another,
In circles of love, we endlessly smother.

Through seasons of change, we hold steadfast true,
With hope as our guide, as we journey anew.
In this radiant circle, our spirits take flight,
Together in devotion, we shine ever bright.

So let us embrace every moment we share,
In circles of love, in the beauty of care.
For together we flourish, with hearts ever free,
In the realm of devotion, our souls blend in glee.

The Tapestry of Grace

In threads of gold, love intertwines,
A gentle touch that redefines.
Each heart a pattern, unique in place,
Bound together by the tapestry of grace.

Through trials faced and shadows cast,
The light of faith holds steadfast.
In every stitch, a story told,
Embracing warmth in hues of gold.

Such beauty blooms where mercy flows,
A garden rich, as kindness grows.
Each moment cherished, a blessing shared,
In the fabric of hope, we are paired.

Together woven, in joy and strife,
The threads of love give meaning to life.
In divine design, we find our role,
Stitched in unity, heart and soul.

Let hearts rejoice and voices raise,
In the melody of life, sing praise.
For in this dance of fate's embrace,
We shine as one in the tapestry of grace.

The Depths of Compassionate Clutch

In the quiet night, a tender sigh,
Compassion flows as stars draw nigh.
Hand in hand, through trials unfold,
We seek the warmth in hearts of gold.

In every struggle, a gentle hold,
A bridge of love where spirits mold.
With every heartbeat, the promise stays,
United we stand, in hopeful ways.

Reach beyond, in pain's embrace,
For every wound, there's a sacred place.
The grip of grace, so strong and tight,
A beacon in the darkest night.

Boundless rivers of mercy spread,
In every tear that's freely shed.
Lifted by hands that understand,
We rise together, heart in hand.

In the depths of love, may we find,
A solace deep and intertwined.
With every struggle, we touch the sky,
In compassionate clutch, we learn to fly.

The Embrace of Sacred Unity

In silent moments, where spirits blend,
A bond unbroken, love transcends.
Each soul a note in harmony,
Together we weave our symphony.

In unity's glow, we face the storm,
Finding shelter, a sacred warm.
In every laugh, in every tear,
The echo of faith draws us near.

Hands joined tight, we rise as one,
In the light of hope, a new day begun.
Through shadows deep, through trials long,
The embrace of unity grows strong.

Majestic skies bear witness to,
The power of love, always true.
With every breath, we celebrate,
In sacred union, we elevate.

One heart, one mind, together we stand,
In the embrace of unity, hand in hand.
For in this bond, fears dissipate,
Our souls unite, we elevate.

The Silent Covenant Among Souls

In whispered moments, our spirits align,
A quiet pact, pure and divine.
Through trials faced, through joy and pain,
The silent covenant shall remain.

In every glance, in every breath,
A promise lives beyond the death.
In shadows cast, in light poured bright,
We walk together, day and night.

With kindness woven in every thread,
A love that lingers, never dead.
In steadfast silence, we rise and fall,
United by grace, we answer the call.

In sacred whispers, we find our way,
Through autumn's chill and spring's bouquet.
The bonds we share, unbreakable, true,
In the silent covenant, me and you.

For every heartbeat, a sacred vow,
In life and death, we honor now.
In the subtle dance of souls that soar,
We find forever, and then some more.

The Pathway of Unseen Light

In shadows deep, our hearts do seek,
A guiding star, a voice to speak.
Through trials faced, we walk in grace,
The unseen light, our sacred place.

With every step, in faith we tread,
The whispers soft, the paths we're led.
Through valleys low, to mountains high,
In silent prayer, we learn to fly.

The road ahead is formed of trust,
In every stone, our hopes adjust.
With open hearts, we share the load,
Embracing love, divine abode.

When burdens weigh upon our soul,
The unseen light will make us whole.
In unity, we rise as one,
In joy and peace, we greet the sun.

Through quiet moments, wisdom calls,
In darkness bright, our spirit sprawls.
The journey's end is but a start,
Where goodness flows, in every heart.

The Breath of Unfaltering Faith

In morning's light, where hopes arise,
We lift our hands, we touch the skies.
With every breath, a prayer takes flight,
Unfaltering faith, our guiding light.

Through storms that rage, we stand secure,
In every doubt, our love is pure.
With hearts aligned, we face the day,
In sacred trust, we find our way.

As rivers flow, so faith will grow,
In gentle whispers, truth we sow.
With each new dawn, our spirits gleam,
In boundless grace, we dare to dream.

In trials faced, we find our strength,
In bonds of love, we go the length.
With every breath, we seek to know,
The depths of faith, that ever flow.

With gratitude, our hearts expand,
In every heartbeat, God's own hand.
We face the world, with joy ablaze,
In breath of faith, all fear we raze.

Grapevines of Grace

In gardens lush, where blessings grow,
Grapevines entwine, a sacred flow.
With heavenly dew, our spirits rise,
In tender care, love never dies.

Through seasons change, our roots run deep,
In faith we strive, in hope we reap.
The bounty shared, a feast divine,
Together, Lord, in love we shine.

With open arms, we gather near,
In every joy, we cast out fear.
The fruits of grace, in harvest spread,
In Christ's embrace, our hearts are fed.

Through trials faced, our bond grows strong,
In unity, we sing our song.
With every vine, a story told,
In love and light, we break the mold.

In gratitude, our hearts we raise,
For grapefinds of grace, eternal praise.
In every leaf, a promise true,
In Christ, our lives, forever new.

The Stillness of the Blessed

In quietude, where wonders bloom,
We find our peace, dispelling gloom.
In stillness, hearts in prayer unite,
The blessed calm, our guiding light.

Amidst the chaos, presence near,
In silence sweet, our God is clear.
With every breath, we feel the grace,
In stillness pure, we seek His face.

Through tranquil nights and dawns so bright,
Our souls ascend, in pure delight.
With gentle love, our worries cease,
In stillness found, our hearts in peace.

As waters flow, in steady stream,
The stillness holds a sacred dream.
With faith embraced, we walk the way,
In blessed moments, come what may.

With humbled hearts, we stand as one,
In stillness shared, our journey's won.
In cherished grace, we're ever blessed,
In quietude, we find our rest.

Nourished by Devotion

In quiet prayer, we seek the light,
A heart in silence, pure and bright.
With every breath, we feel the grace,
In sacred union, we find our place.

From shutters closed, our spirits soar,
With faith, we open every door.
In sacred texts, our souls intertwine,
Nourished by love, divine design.

Each act of kindness, a holy seed,
In giving, we fulfill the need.
Among the flowers of His will,
Our hearts are filled, our thirst is still.

Through trials faced, we rise again,
Finding strength in holy kin.
With every tear, a blessing flows,
In letting go, true faith grows.

Around the table, prayers are shared,
In cherished moments, souls laid bare.
With every story, a reason found,
In love's embrace, we are unbound.

Amongst the Celestial

Stars above in endless night,
Whispers soft, a guiding light.
In sacred spaces, dreams take flight,
Amongst the celestial, pure delight.

Angels sing, their voices clear,
In harmony, we draw them near.
Each glowing orb tells tales of love,
A gift bestowed from realms above.

Moonlight dances on the lake,
Caressing waters, hearts awake.
In silver beams, we find our prayer,
In silent trust, a bond we share.

Clouds drift by, a fleeting view,
In gentle breezes, mercy true.
With every sunset, blessings flow,
In twilight's calm, our spirits grow.

Amongst the stars, we find our song,
In unity, we all belong.
An endless choir, voices raised,
In worship sweet, our hearts amazed.

The Power of Presence

In every moment, silence speaks,
In presence felt, our spirit seeks.
With open hearts, we gather near,
In gentle hugs, we cast out fear.

The power of touch, a holy balm,
In tender whispers, peace is calm.
A gaze that lingers, love defined,
In every smile, our souls aligned.

From chaos born, we draw the still,
In sacred pauses, bend the will.
In lessons learned, we rise anew,
With faith as anchor, hope shines through.

In simple acts of kindness shown,
A harvest gathered, seeds well sown.
With every laugh, a hymn released,
In joyful hearts, we find our feast.

To be present is to believe,
In quiet love, our souls conceive.
In every heartbeat, hear the call,
With presence shared, we rise, we fall.

Unbroken Bonds

In family ties, a sacred thread,
Through trials faced, our love is spread.
With laughter shared, the joy unmasks,
In unity, a bond that lasts.

Through storms we weather, hand in hand,
In every heartbeat, we understand.
With patience shown, and grace renewed,
In every challenge, love imbued.

For distance cannot sever ties,
In every prayer, our spirit rises.
Through whispered dreams, our voices blend,
In every letter, love transcends.

The roots we plant, in soil divine,
In cherished memories, our hearts entwine.
Through laughter and tears, together we stand,
In love's embrace, life's gentle hand.

With every story shared, we grow,
In legacy, our love will flow.
Unbroken bonds, forever true,
In heart and spirit, me and you.

Horizons of Faithful Longing

Beneath the skies so vast and bright,
Our hearts reach out to grace and light.
In whispers soft, the spirits call,
Guiding our steps through shadows tall.

Through valleys deep and mountains high,
We seek the truth as days go by.
Each prayer a beacon, shining clear,
In every doubt, our faith draws near.

The dawn awakens with gentle sighs,
Restoring hope as darkness flies.
With every breath, a promise made,
In every heart, our trust displayed.

We gather strength from those who've gone,
Their love a light, a steadfast dawn.
Across the miles, our spirits blend,
In sacred bonds that never end.

So let us rise, together stand,
Embracing faith, hand in hand.
With every step, the journey bold,
Horizons vast, our dreams unfold.

The Quietude of Hope's Assurance

In stillness found, where shadows play,
The heart finds peace, the soul's own way.
A tranquil dawn begins to break,
With whispers soft, our spirits wake.

Beneath the stars, the night does breathe,
A promise held, in faith we weave.
The echo of a prayer so sweet,
Embracing all, as hearts entreat.

Each moment holds a silent grace,
In quietude, we find our place.
Through trials faced, and storms that rage,
Hope's gentle light, a sacred page.

Together we stand, in unity strong,
With every heartbeat, we belong.
A tapestry of love entwined,
In hope's assurance, we are blind.

So trust the path, though steep and wild,
In every heart, God's promise smiles.
Through silent prayers and gentle dreams,
The quietude of hope redeems.

Gathered Together in Reverence

In sacred spaces, spirits rise,
With open hearts, we lift our eyes.
Each voice a song, a sweet refrain,
In reverence, we find our gain.

Hands united, in purpose strong,
Together we hum a timeless song.
Through trials faced, we'll not despair,
For in this bond, we're held with care.

The stories shared, in joy and tears,
Each moment shared, dispelling fears.
In love's embrace, we find our grace,
Together moving, a sacred place.

With every breath, we honor the past,
The light we share, forever cast.
As one we stand, a steadfast clan,
In faith renewed, in joy we span.

So let us gather, hearts ablaze,
In reverence for all our days.
For in each other, we find the flame,
Gathered together, calling His name.

Resilient Threads of the Spirit

In fabric woven, love entwined,
Resilient threads, our hearts aligned.
Through every storm, we shall not break,
In faith's embrace, a path we make.

With courage bold, we face the day,
Each challenge met, we choose to pray.
In trials faced, our spirits soar,
Resilient threads, forevermore.

The journey long, with twists and turns,
In every heart, the fire burns.
With gentle whispers, spirits fly,
Through every sorrow, love stands by.

So lift your hearts, and trust the way,
For in His light, we find our stay.
With every step, the future bright,
Resilient threads, unite in light.

Together we sew, with threads of grace,
In every stitch, His warm embrace.
In unity strong, we rise and sing,
Resilient threads, our spirits cling.

Milton Keynes UK
Ingram Content Group UK Ltd.
UKHW020039271124
451585UK00012B/934